Romanza

The California Architecture of Frank Lloyd Wright

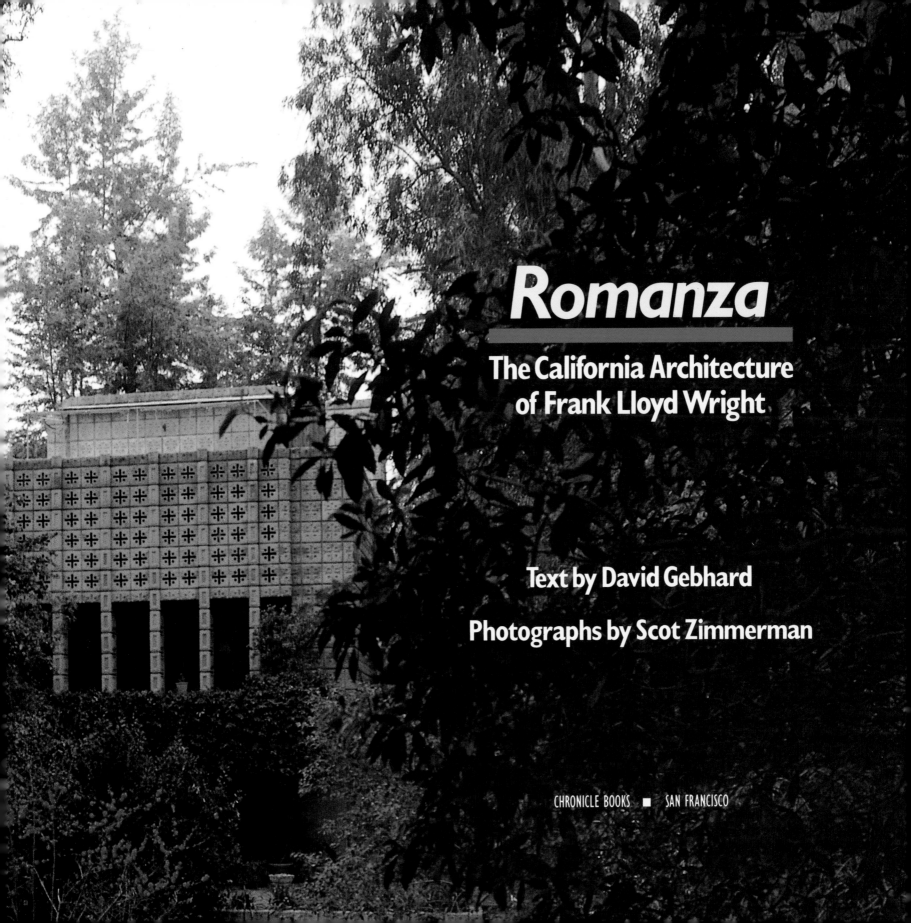

Romanza

The California Architecture of Frank Lloyd Wright

Text by David Gebhard

Photographs by Scot Zimmerman

CHRONICLE BOOKS ■ SAN FRANCISCO

Printed in Japan.

Library of Congress
Cataloging-in-Publication Data

Gebhard, David.
    Romanza: The California Architecture of
        Frank Lloyd Wright
    Bibliography: p.
    Includes index.
    1. Wright, Frank Lloyd, 1867–1959—
Criticism and interpretation. 2. Architecture
and climate—California. 3. Organic
architecture—California. 4. Architecture,
Modern—20th century—California. I. Wright,
Frank Lloyd, 1867–1959. II. Zimmerman, Scot.
III. Title.
NA737.W7G43 1988   720'.92'4   87–10290
ISBN 0–87701–379–9

Editing: Frankie Wright
Design: Seventeenth Street Studios
Composition: Another Point, Inc.

Distributed in Canada by Raincoast Books
112 East 3rd Avenue
Vancouver, B.C. V5T 1C8

10 9 8 7 6 5 4 3

Chronicle Books
275 Fifth Street
San Francisco, California 94103

CONTENTS

Preface — 1

George C. Stewart house
1909
196 Hot Springs Road
Montecito, Santa Barbara — 8

**Aline Barnsdall house
(Hollyhock House)**
1917–1921
Barnsdall Park, Hollywood Boulevard
and Vermont Avenue, Hollywood — 12

**Alice Millard house
(La Miniatura)**
1923
645 Prospect Crescent
Pasadena — 18

Charles Ennis house
1923–1924
2607 Glendower Avenue
Los Feliz District, Los Angeles — 22

John Storer house
1923–1924
8161 Hollywood Boulevard
Hollywood — 28

Samuel Freeman house
1923–1924
1962 Glencoe Way
Hollywood — 32

**Paul R. and Jean S. Hanna house
(Honeycomb House)**
1936
737 Frenchmans Road
Stanford — 36

Sidney Bazett house
1938–1940
101 Reservoir Road
Hillsborough — 42

George D. Sturges house | 1939 | 48
449 Skyeway Drive
Brentwood Heights, Los Angeles

Arch Oboler Gatehouse | 1940, 1941 | 52
and Studio-Retreat | 32436 Mulholland Drive
Malibu

Mrs. Clinton Walker house | 1948 | 58
Scenic Road at Martin Street
Carmel

Maynard P. Buehler house | 1948 | 62
6 Great Oak Circle
Orinda

V. C. Morris Gift Shop | 1949 | 66
140 Maiden Lane
San Francisco

Robert Berger house | 1950 | 70
259 Redwood Road
San Anselmo

Arthur C. Mathews house | 1950 | 74
83 Wisteria Way
Atherton

Wilbur C. Pearce house | 1950 | 78
5 Bradbury Hills Road
Bradbury

Anderton Court Shops | 1952 | 84
322 North Rodeo Drive
Beverly Hills

Karl Kundert Medical Clinic | 1954–1956 | 88
1106 Pacific Street
San Luis Obispo

Randall Fawcett house   1955   92
                                   21200 Center Avenue
                                   Los Banos

Robert G. Walton house   1957   98
                                   417 Rogue Road
                                   Modesto

George Ablin house   1958   104
                                   2460 Country Club Drive
                                   Bakersfield

Marin County Civic Center   1957–1972   110
                                   North San Pedro Road
                                   at U.S. Highway 101
                                   San Rafael

Pilgrim Congregational Church 1958–1963   116
                                   2850 Foothill Boulevard
                                   Redding

Hilary and Joe Feldman house   1974   120
                                   13 Mosswood Road
                                   Berkeley

                                   Unbuilt Projects   125

                                   Related Sources   129

                                   References   131

                                   Index   133

I n discussing Frank Lloyd Wright's work of the 1920s in Southern California, Lloyd Wright mentioned that there were four facets of the place that intrigued his father. These were its sense of being a desert susceptible to transformation through the introduction of water, the factual and mythical relation of the place to a primitive pre-European past, the loose horizontal spread, which even in 1920 characterized Los Angeles and its satellite communities, and then the way all of this could be experienced (and in a sense be brought into reality) by a passionate commitment to the private automobile. These reactions on Wright's part governed much of his work in California during the twenties. From the thirties on he increasingly saw in California a place where his ideal of the auto-oriented horizontal city might be realized. How Wright did or did not maneuver his California projects within his grand scheme of varied regionalism and of the horizontal dispersed city provides an insight into the several decades of his work in this state.

Opposite: Charles Ennis house. This page: Aline Barnsdall house (Hollyhock).

Wright's first building in California, the George C. Stewart house of 1909 in Montecito, illustrates the "game" he often played in choosing between a design that was specific to the client and regionally appropriate and one that was a generalized product likely to appear almost anywhere under a variety of guises. The Stewart house is a characteristic two-story cruciform Prairie Style dwelling one might encounter in the suburbs of Chicago or on the shores of a Wisconsin lake; only here it is placed in an entirely different environment—in a coastal community that overlooks the Pacific and enjoys a year-round mild climate. Whatever Wright's vision may have been of the environment and the site, he clearly felt strongly enough about his design to include a beautiful perspective drawing of it in his famous 1910 Wasmuth portfolio (Studies and Executed Buildings by Frank Lloyd Wright). Curiously, the drawing accurately reflects the principal vegetation and contours of the site, but he mistakenly captions the house as being located in Fresno, an inland community in the San Joaquin Valley where the climate is decidedly different from that of coastal California.

Though Wright in his autobiography sarcastically wrote about his fellow midwesterners simply transplanting Iowa to California, one senses that even this gifted and perceptive individual never fully shed his own midwestern-inspired quixotic views of California and the Southwest. In his fifty years plus of designing for California, Wright shifted back and forth between an urge to be

Above: drawing, George C. Stewart house. Below: Alice Millard house.

regional and a seeming desire to see buildings realized that were variations on themes he had developed for locales all across the country. Of his California work (twenty-four realized buildings; over thirty unrealized projects), it could well be argued that more often than not his most successful designs were those in which he consciously sought to express a regional flavor, a flavor having more to do with the spirit of the place and the society that occupied it than any outright cultivation of environmental or historical linkage.

In 1931, having by then completed several projects in Southern California, Wright wrote of his reaction to California and its cultivated Hispanic architectural tradition: "We have had with us dead things that we have sentimentally taken as live traditions . . . [one of] which Father Junipero brought up from Mexico into California, Southwest." Perhaps thinking of the elegantly simple geometric stucco houses of San Diego architect Irving J. Cill or of such exponents of the Spanish Colonial Revival as Santa Barbara's George Washington Smith, with his almost primitive versions of the Andalusian farmhouses of Spain, Wright commended the creation of simple, white-surfaced buildings, which gain a richness through their contrast with the wide palette of native and introduced plants. Though he approved of this approach to designing in California, he never adopted such an abstract, unembellished approach himself.

In two realized buildings after the Stewart house, the Barnsdall house in Hollywood (1917–1920) and the Millard house in Pasadena (1923), the architect sought to "one-up" the widely acclaimed borrowing of Hispanic sources for structures in California by going back to the more distant past of pre-Columbian Mexico. The "primitive" architecture of the Mayans and the Zapotecs provided Wright with an image through which he could fight a number of visual and ideological battles. Because the source originated in the Americas, Wright could emphasize the independence of the New World from Europe. As a historical form associated with Mexico, and by implication with the Hispanic sections of the American Southwest and Southern California, this image gave an appearance of being natural and "organic" to the place; it represented a historically logical response to the physical and climatic environment of California and the Southwest. Wright's recourse to the pre-Columbian also accommodated his participation in the open romanticism so prevalent in the then fashionable Period Revival architecture. Throughout his life Wright persistently denied being influenced by any architecture, past or present, but his borrowings were as intense and as varied as any of his contemporaries. The difference, though, between Wright and other architects of his time has to do with the way in which he transformed borrowed forms and absorbed them into his own architectural language.

Wright had long been intrigued with pre-Columbian architecture. (While working for Adler and Sullivan on their Transportation Building at the 1893 World Columbian Exposition in Chicago,

he saw a partial reconstruction of the Mayan Nunnery of Uxmal and other Mayan buildings.) His enthusiasm for this architecture strongly came into the open at first, not in any "indigenous" designs for California and the Southwest, but in two seemingly unlikely building types situated in equally unlikely places: the A. D. German Warehouse in the small rural community of Richland Center, Wisconsin (1915), and his extravaganza of a beer garden, the Midway Gardens in Chicago (1914). In these two projects he adapted the Mayan compositional approach of an ornamental band placed above a plain masonry surface. The bands of geometric motifs, realized in concrete, were inspired directly from Mayan and Zapotec examples.

The first California commission to display this Mayan primitivism was the Hollyhock House, built for Aline Barnsdall on Hollywood's Olive Hill. In his complex design, Wright took this pre-Columbian ingredient and mingled it with his earlier use of the Beaux Arts-derived cruciform plan, together with a siting and landscaping suggestive of the approach often taken in the Classic Mediterranean country houses of his Beaux Arts rival, Charles A. Platt. The house was to be the centerpiece for an extensive community of buildings, including a theater, artists' living and studio quarters, a kindergarten, garden structures, and other secondary houses. Two of these smaller houses were built, but the remainder of the project was never realized.

Even more grandiose in extent and concept, and inspired from many sources, was Wright's unrealized project for the Doheny Ranch Development above Sierra Madre (1921). The siting of these houses with their walled gardens is reminiscent of the groupings of Tuscan villas Wright had experienced during his stay near Florence when he was working on the drawings for his 1910 Wasmuth portfolio. But the actual design of each of these concrete houses is pure pre-Columbian.

Several of the mountainside villas of precast concrete block depicted in drawings for this project served as a basis for his four realized precast concrete block houses of 1923 and 1924. Concrete, concrete block, and cement stucco sheathing had been viewed by Wright and other architects of the years after 1900 as the new materials for domestic architecture. Concrete (and its related structural forms) was actually taken up by many California architects, all of whom inevita-

bly had to deal with questions of how to use it and how to express its use in the design of buildings. In California, Wright's response (as well as that of his son Lloyd) was to look to concrete block construction. Concrete block both expressed this new material and, through indirect historical associations, connected it to the region.

All four Southern California precast concrete block houses pose in one way or another as symbolic romantic ruins: the Millard house (1923) peeks forth from its "jungle" pool and thick vegetation, the Freeman (1923) and Storer houses (1923–1924) nearly disappear into steep, vegetation-enshrouded hillsides, and the dramatic Ennis house (1923–1924) stands as an abstraction of a Mayan temple perched on a hilltop.

Wright argued that buildings in Southern California should ". . . grow

right out of the soil wherever sand and gravel abound. . . . " An open sympathy indeed exists between the color of the soil and the color of his concrete blocks, but this ends up as only a minor note because the landscape surrounding these houses was radically transformed into a junglelike screen of vegetation (often from the landscape designs of Lloyd Wright). What one is really aware of, from a distance or close up, is the assertive forms of each building and the strong shadows cast by the deep geometric patterning of the block. Wright scathingly denounced the architectural designs of his contemporaries, yet these Southern California houses are not only avidly romantic, they are also theatrical and exotic, closely akin to other buildings then being built in Los Angeles, whether Neo-Babylonian or Neo-Islamic. In the early thirties when Wright, in one of his

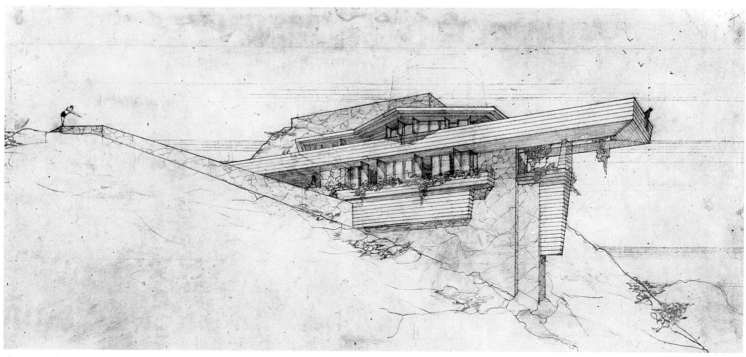

Opposite: drawing, Doheny Ranch, unbuilt. Above: drawing, Arch Oboler house, "Eagle Feather", unbuilt.

characteristically petulant moods, said that "houses in California—Mexican, Hispanic, and Hopi—are more atrocious than skyscrapers in New York," San Francisco architect Bernard Maybeck responded by commenting that houses such as these fulfill dreams. Maybeck could easily have gone on to observe that Wright's own work of the twenties in California was as romantically dreamlike as any dwellings with Spanish or Mediterranean influences.

With Wright's ideological and visual sensitivity to environment, it is surprising that during these years in the late teens and twenties he seemed to have generally viewed the whole of coastal Southern California as simply an extension of the inland deserts of California and Arizona. His designs for several unrealized projects for the Salt River Valley of Arizona

are essentially similar to those he built or projected for the Los Angeles region. He did, however, make much more of a distinction between Northern and Southern California as expressed in his designs for the Lake Tahoe Summer Colony (1922), another of his many unbuilt California projects. Here the woodsy nature of the North is reflected in the forms and materials used in a colony of lakeshore cabins and houseboats.

From this point on, Wright's forms are more difficult to view as singularly regional. It could, perhaps, be suggested that the theatrics of Wright's unbuilt Sports Club for Huntington Hartford (seemingly a nest of flying saucers moored to a masonry mast) in the Hollywood Hills (1947), the projected V. C. Morris house (overhanging the Pacific from a high cliff) near San Francisco

(1946), or the earlier project for Arch Oboler near Malibu (1940) reflect the agitated, stuccolike "Hollywood" atmosphere of Southern California; but a look through Wright's concurrent work designed for locations in the Midwest and East indicates that these California schemes, while almost always specifically site oriented, were not regionally oriented. The same holds true for other major California designs: the Paul R. Hanna house at Stanford (1936), the George D. Sturges house in Brentwood Heights (1940), the projected Stuart Haldron house, Carmel (1945), and the V. C. Morris Gift Shop in San Francisco (1948). These are rightly considered landmarks in twentieth century American architecture, but they could just as well have been built in rural Wisconsin or New England. Wright's California houses of the post-World War II years were sometimes a variation on his pre-World War II midwestern Usonian houses (Wright's own version of the single floor California ranch house); on other occasions in their siting, plans, and materials, they are clearly related to forms he developed in the twenties and thirties as a response to the Arizona and California desert regions.

In a number of ways the Marin County Civic Center (1957–1972) may be seen as Wright's final comment on California and the interplay between his ideal of "organic" regionalism and the universalism of his own architectural language. The Marin County buildings suggest that his advocacy of decentralization, of the desirability of creating horizontal cities, and the mobility provided by the automobile (expressed abstractly in his paper scheme for Broadacre City in 1934 and later) could be attained in California. In 1932, Wright posed the question "Which would you give up first, the city or the automobile, if you had to choose between moving away into more ordered green spaciousness to keep your mobilization or remain on 'the hard,' in the herd, where you must eventually give it up." Though grossly imperfect, as Wright continually pointed out, California from the twenties on held out a regional possibility of actually fulfilling his dream

HOUSE FOR HUNTINGTON HARTFORD
FRANK LLOYD WRIGHT ARCHITECT
LLOYD WRIGHT ASSOCIATE

COUNTRY CLUB FOR HUNTINGTON HARTFORD HOLLYW
FRANK LLOYD WRIGHT ARCHITECT

of Broadacre City, with its low density Usonian middle-class suburban dwellings, its dispersal of business, industry, and public institutions, and its potential for evolving its own regional architectural language. Coupling together his earlier planning schemes for Olive Hill in Los Angeles and the Doheny Ranch with the siting of the Marin County Civic Center offers a fragmented glimpse of Wright's view of California and its potential.

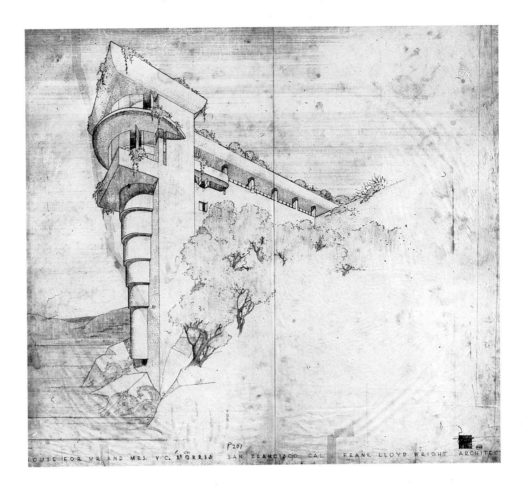

Opposite above: drawing, Huntington Hartford house, unbuilt. Below: drawing Huntington Hartford Sports Club, unbuilt. This page above: signature tile from George Ablin house. Above right: drawing, V. C. Morris house, unbuilt. Below: Marin Civic Center.

GEORGE C. STEWART HOUSE

The woodsy redwood-sheathed Stewart house was Wright's first realized commission on the West Coast. Wright completed the design in his Oak Park studio only months before his notorious trip to Europe with Mamah Borthwick Cheney. The avowed purpose of Wright's trip to Europe was to prepare the drawings for his famed portfolio published in Berlin in 1910 by Ernest Wasmuth. After his rather sudden departure, apparently neither the Wright office nor Marion Mahoney Griffin and Herman von Holst, who took on the uncompleted commissions, supervised construction of the house, and numerous design changes were made. Perhaps because it was such a recent project, Wright felt strongly enough about the design to include an impressive perspective drawing of it in the Wasmuth portfolio.

The accentuate horizontal board and batten exterior and the simplicity of interior detailing reflect the general approach Wright had often taken to lakeshore summer houses in southern Wisconsin, especially the Charles S. Ross house of 1902, and to the clubhouse and cottages designed in 1910 for the partially realized Como Orchard Colony (Darby, Montana).

The cruciform plan, with its two-story living room and the pair of second floor cantilevered sleeping balconies, recalls many of his midwestern suburban and lakeshore Prairie designs of 1900 through 1909. The Stewart house is essentially a Prairie house, transplanted unchanged to a radically different environment—the southern California coast.

Some changes were made in Wright's design during construction, and shortly afterwards the two-story service wing was substantially altered. The service wing was enlarged, the attached garage became the kitchen, and the second floor sleeping balconies were enclosed in glass. And since construction, vegetation in this section of Montecito has grown to the point that the house no longer enjoys a view to the ocean through its own (non-native) pine forest. Despite the changes, the strength of the original design remains, especially in the grand space of the living room and its axial projection into the adjoining lower space of the reception room and the dining room. Whereas Wright continued to employ many Prairie elements in his subsequent California work, these features tended to be absorbed into his later interests to create a new form of regionalism.

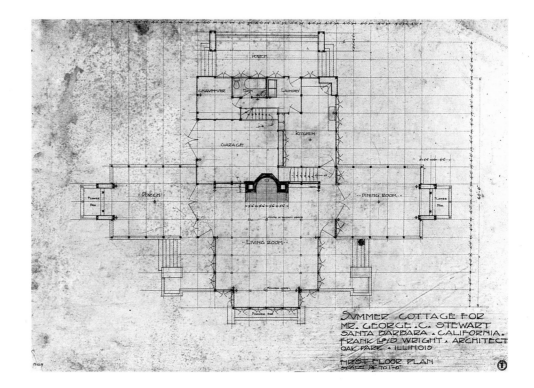

ALINE
BARNSDALL
HOUSE
(HOLLYHOCK
HOUSE)

Certainly the most widely known of Wright's West Coast designs is the Barnsdall house atop Olive Hill in the eastern section of Hollywood. Here, situated on a high hill and surrounded by olive trees and others, stands the concrete house, which, as it was pointed out in 1941, "recalls the massive temples of the Aztecs." And indeed the smooth masonry mass of the building, its highly stylized pattern of hollyhocks, and its upwardly projecting pinnacles does illustrate Wright's long interest in primitive non-European forms. In the case of the Hollyhock House (as Wright labeled it), the pre-Columbian architectural influence is not of the Aztecs, but that of the Mayans.

To Wright, Southern California, which he looked upon as part of the American Southwest, seemed the most logical place to receive a primitive historical transplant from Mexico and Guatemala. In many ways the Hollyhock House, and the Los Angeles group of precast concrete block houses of the twenties, were Wright's personal response, his answer to ideas of historicism and regionalism in California.

The readability of these Los Angeles buildings as being openly inspired by historical precedent has always been recognized; only, of course, Wright abstracted it all and came up with a version that was decidedly his own. His historicism had an atmosphere of unreality—as if it were straight from the illustrated pages of a children's adventure book of the time.

In a series of writings of the late 1920s, "In the Cause of Architecture," Wright devoted a chapter to the uses of concrete, noting that it is more truly an artificial stone than it is anything else. Accompanying this chapter were illustrations of the Barnsdall house, Wright's version of modern, twentieth century "cast stone," a product used widely by American architects from the early

1900s through the 1920s. Though the house poses as a monolithic concrete building, its structure ranges from the use of reinforced concrete to hollow tile, even to stucco-covered wood studs. Wright created not the fact of a monolithic concrete building, but the illusion of one (and an impressive illusion it is), much in the manner of his colleagues, the traditionalists, whom he repeatedly chastised for their lack of "honesty" in the use of materials and structure.

In the same series of writings, Wright asserted: "There is more beauty in a fine ground plan than in almost any of its ultimate consequences." This primacy of the plan illustrates his hidden but fundamental adherence to many of the essential design principles of the French Ecole de Beaux Arts. The Hollyhock House

beautifully illustrates this adherence on Wright's part to a tradition he supposedly opposed. The main public rooms of the house—entrance loggia, living room, music room, and library—are organized in a classic T-shaped form, with the major axis going through the loggia and living room, countered by a secondary cross axis of the music room and library. This was a device Wright had frequently used in many of his Midwest Prairie houses of the early 1900s, however, he added a walled patio off to the south and two extended wings enclosing a garden court. And as he had often done with his suburban Chicago houses, he treated the entrance as a mysterious affair. One enters through a long, narrow loggia, which in turn leads into a deep cavelike entry.

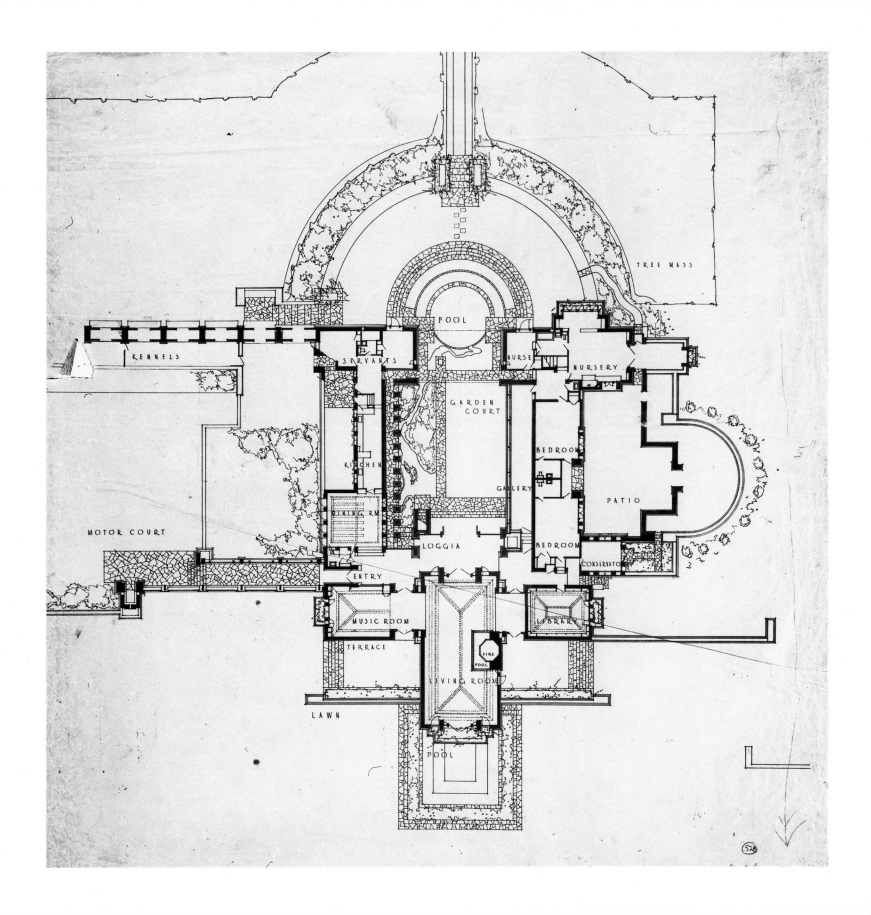

KENNELS

SERVANTS

POOL

NURSE

NURSERY

GARDEN COURT

TREE MASS

KITCHEN

GALLERY

BEDROOM

PATIO

MOTOR COURT

DINING RM

LOGGIA

BEDROOM

CONSERVATORY

ENTRY

FIRE POOL

MUSIC ROOM

LIBRARY

TERRACE

LIVING ROOM

LAWN

POOL

52ͦ

The Hollyhock House itself was meant to be only one component, the Mayan "temple" on top of the hill, around which were to be grouped other dwellings, studios, a theater, and so on, all part of an extensive self-contained artists' colony. Aline Barnsdall sought to promote an idealized form of socialism, and Olive Hill was to be a realization of this new world. In addition to the house, only two peripheral residences were built, residences "A" and "B," as well as a hillside pergola and children's wading pool. (Residence B, the pergola, and wading pool survive.)

The actual on-site supervision of the construction was under the direction of R. M. Schindler, who later became one of America's most intriguing Modernist architects. Schindler designed the A and B residences and was joined by another young Austrian exponent of European Modernism, Richard J. Neutra, to design the wading pool and pergola (1925). The landscaping of Olive Hill, which regrettably was never fully carried out, was the work of Lloyd Wright.

In 1927 Aline Barnsdall deeded Olive Hill and its buildings to the City of Los Angeles; since then it has been a public park, and the house is open to the public. The house was restored in the 1970s, originally under the direction of Lloyd Wright.

ALICE
MILLARD
HOUSE
(LA MINIATURA)

The combined dwelling and bookstudio for Alice Millard was Wright's first realized textured concrete block house on the West Coast. "Concrete is a plastic material," wrote Wright in An Autobiography, "susceptible to the impressions of the imagination." La Miniatura turned out to be the most openly romantic of his concrete block houses of the twenties. The dwelling's location, within a low ravine, enshrouded by trees, and overlooking a pond with a path of stepping stones across it, created a highly potent poetic image, similar to that of Falling Water poised over its waterfall at Bear Run, Pennsylvania (1936).

The north side of the house is placed directly adjacent to a small lane; one enters through a paved court leading to an entry covered by a low bridge that spans from the house to the roof terrace over the garage. The interior boasts a two-story living room with a high window wall composed of glass doors at the lower level and a pattern of perforated concrete blocks above. The walls of thin concrete blocks, with an air space between, occur both externally and internally, thus tying the inside closely to the outdoors. The block pattern with a sunken central cross suggests the legendary pre-Columbian architecture of Mitla near Oaxaca in southern Mexico. But as in all of Wright's work, the historical reference, while present, has been transformed into something modern; in this instance, the massiveness of pre-Columbian masonry has been maneuvered into a light-feeling, open perforated shell.

Wright had originally designed a studio addition to the southwest of the main house, which was eventually designed and carried out in 1926 by his son Lloyd.

The knitblock system of concrete block that Wright employed had been discussed and experimented with by Wright himself, his son Lloyd, and his former associate of Oak Park days, Walter Burley Griffin. The system consisted of two parallel rows of four-inch thick block separated by an air cavity. Steel reinforcing rod was used at intervals to tie these two walls together and to reinforce the walls both horizontally and vertically. Some blocks had a smooth face, others were patterned, and some had their patterns projected through the block. Glass was added internally to the fully perforated block.

In all of his Los Angeles block houses Wright used sand from the site for his concrete mix; his argument being that the color and texture of the concrete surface would be indigenous to the site. As Lloyd Wright commented many years later, this was a logical organic approach, but in fact it had several drawbacks: the natural color and texture of the block did not end up mirroring the site, and because it was close to impossible to wash impurities out of the local sand, the blocks have not been too stable over time.

CHARLES
ENNIS
HOUSE

Wright's 1923 Millard house, the still earlier German Warehouse (Richland Center, Wisconsin, 1915), and his famous Midway Gardens (Chicago, 1914) had revealed his long-time fascination with America's pre-Columbian past. In the siting and design of the Ennis house, however, Wright went the furthest in revealing his attachment to the pre-Columbian architecture of Mexico and Central America. This house, with its extensive layering of textured and plain concrete block retaining walls and parapeted towers, does indeed invoke a twentieth century version of a Mayan temple looking out from the summit of its own mountain. The alternating bands of block walls, stepped back successively from bottom to top, suggest the pyramided platforms of an archaeological site one might suddenly come upon in the jungles of Yucatan or Honduras, or better yet in the romantic illustrations of Frederick Catherwood in John L. Stephens' widely read 1841 Incidents of Travel in Central America.

Once on the hill, however, the temple illusion fades, replaced by a low, horizontal massing, vaguely reminiscent of the palace structure at the Toltec site of Mitla in southern Mexico. Within, the corridored spaces seem endless; Wright must certainly have been thinking in terms of the romantic mystery of a Hollywood film set. In his autobiography he speaks of the house as "the little palace," crowning a high ridge. Regardless of size, and this house is monumental, Wright's work is inevitably dramatic. In this case the drama is heightened by the Hollywood location and associations one makes with the film world of the twenties.

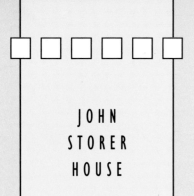

JOHN STORER HOUSE

*T*he Storer house was the second of Wright's Los Angeles textured concrete block houses. Though its form, terrace walls, and textured block are loosely pre-Columbian, and similar to the Ennis house of the same year, the house's essential quality has more in common with the many distinguished southern California Period houses designed at the time by Reginald D. Johnson, George Washington Smith, Gordon Kaufmann, and others. The scale of the living room and the way in which it gains its views through vertical bands of glass share many points of similarity to such Los Angeles houses of the twenties as Bernard Maybeck's medieval Hispanic castle, the Earl C. Anthony house (1927), located in the nearby Los Feliz district; the entrance and garden terraces are planned in a fashion similar to that of a Spanish or Mediterranean image house of the teens or twenties.

In design, the central, high living room mass emerges as a rectangular volume set far back from its surrounding terraces. The wings to each side (bedrooms to the west, service to the east), because of their low scale, help reinforce the dominance and verticality of the central pavilion. Lloyd Wright supervised construction and, as the landscape architect, provided an illusion that this terraced composition should be seen as a fragment, almost a ruin, just barely visible within its "jungle" environment. Some restoration of the house was carried out in the early 1970s by Lloyd Wright; the restoration has been completed by Lloyd's son Eric Wright and by Martin Eli Weil.

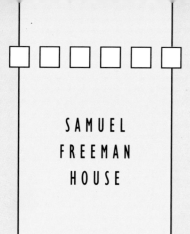

SAMUEL
FREEMAN
HOUSE

T he Freeman house was the last
of Wright's concrete block
houses of the twenties in the Los
Angeles area. At approximately 1200
square feet, it is the smallest, but is in
many ways the most adventurous of
them all. In responding to the needs of
the Freemans and to a small precipitous
site, Wright realized a concrete block
dwelling that was light, airy, and deli-
cate, aspects not usually associated with
this material. The abundant use of perforated block, with glass often set within,
and the breaking of the corners of the
building with extensive glass openings
are highly successful in suggesting an
intimate domestic scale. Internally and
externally, the design of the metal mul-
lions of the windows, which follow the
patterning of the adjoining block walls,
encourages a response to the concrete
walls as thin screens, rather than as solid
heavy masonry planes. R. M. Schindler's
free-standing and built-in furniture,
designed and built in the 1920s and
1930s, reinforces this linear, domestic
quality, particularly in the commitment
to the horizontal. Lloyd Wright supervised the construction of the house, and
certainly his background as a landscape
architect contributed to the way in which
the house and its terraces and walls disappear into the hillside.

The house plays off a rich variety of precedents that intrigued Wright: the pre-Columbian merges into the Islamic (perforated screens reminiscent of those encountered in Moghal architecture); concrete is transformed into the thin delicacy and open interior horizontality associated with the traditional Japanese house.

In 1984, Harriet Press Freeman, who with her husband had commissioned the house, gave it and an endowment for its maintenance to the University of Southern California. When restoration is complete, the house will be open on occasion to the public.

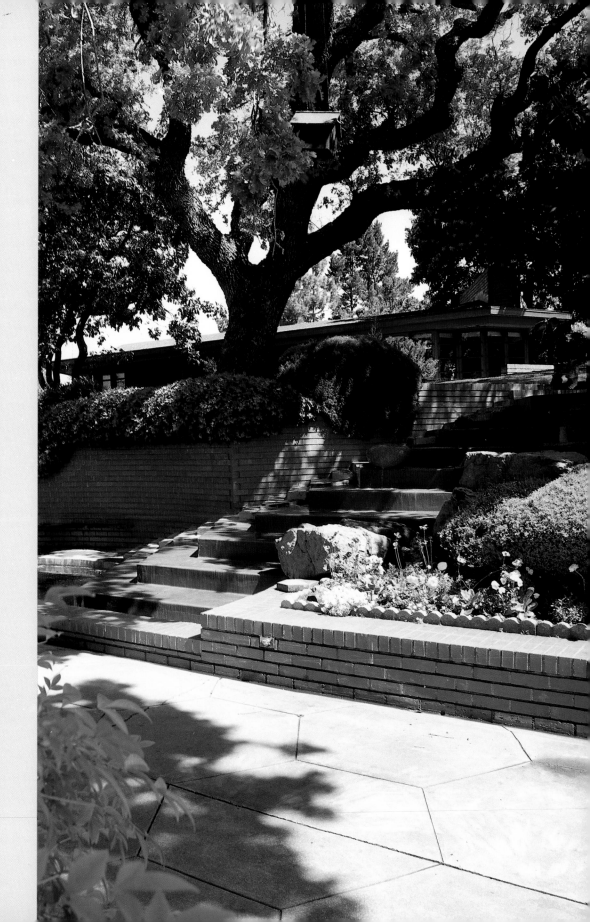

PAUL R. AND JEAN S. HANNA HOUSE (HONEYCOMB HOUSE)

The year 1936, in the midst of the Great Depression, stands as a singular high point in the career of Wright. He dramatically reasserted his preeminence on the international architectural scene with a remarkable compendium of buildings: Falling Water at Bear Run, Pennsylvania for the Kaufmann family; the Administration Building of the Johnson Wax Company in Racine, Wisconsin; the first Jacobs house in Madison (his first Usonian house); and finally the Honeycomb House near Stanford University.

Like Wright's own Taliesin at Spring Green, Wisconsin, the Hanna house snuggles into the side of a gently sloping hill. A walled garden, the entrance auto court, and the separate garage and study guest wing tie the house to the inner hillside. On the other side, brick terraces provide additional outdoor living space and splendid views of the countryside.

The Hanna house was Wright's first house in the Bay Area. Though in a suburban situation, it poses, as was frequently the case with his houses, as a rural country house. The modular concept of this house is that of the repeated hexagon (the honeycomb), arranged to create a remarkable openness of plan and to project the various interior spaces outward onto adjoining terraces and views. In 1938, when the house was published in the Architectural Record, Wright wrote that he used the hexagon because it was more economical than the usual rectangle, that it was consistent with "a more human rhythm." Elaborating, he stated, "All corners are obtuse as in the honeycombs, therefore a pattern more natural to human movement is the result."

Interior vertical space of the house is complex. The high central clearstory is played off against the low roofs and ceiling, which define the perimeter of the building. Externally, brick has been used to solidly "ground" the dwelling to its hillside site. Thin walls composed of layered laminated wood were designed so that many could be moved and rearranged. Thus, when the Hanna's children had grown up, their section of the house was replanned for new needs.

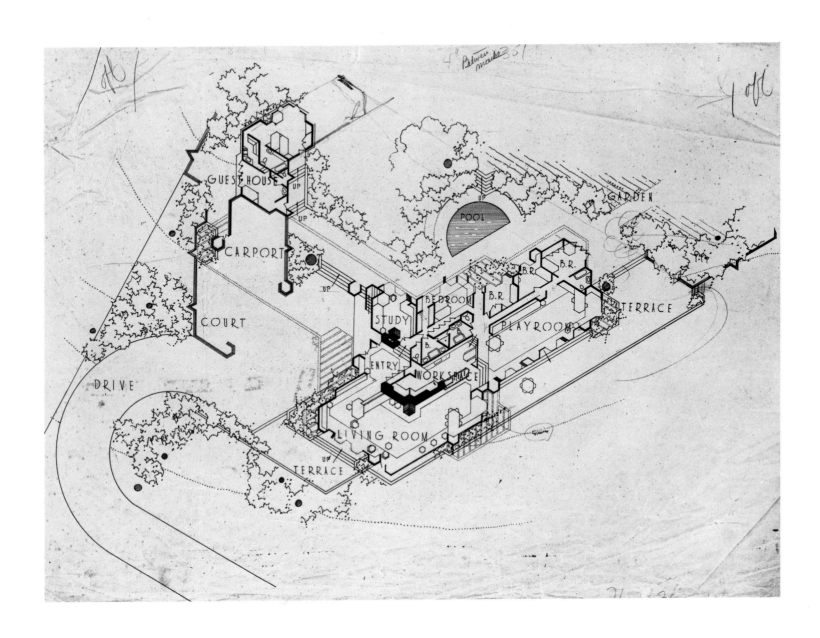

GUEST HOUSE

GARDEN

CARPORT

POOL

B.R.

B.R.

B.R.

TERRACE

COURT

BEDROOM

STUDY

PLAYROOM

ENTRY

WORKSPACE

DRIVE

LIVING ROOM

TERRACE

TERRACE

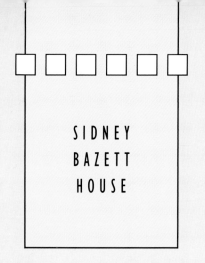

SIDNEY
BAZETT
HOUSE

*T*he Sidney Bazett house continues the use of the hexagonal module Wright had so successfully applied a few years before in the nearby Hanna house. As in the Hanna house, the lower sections of the walls are brick with accentuated raked horizontal joints; the upper portions of the walls and the roof are of laminated redwood. The in-and-out-again quality of the small horizontal mullioned glass bays and walls suggests that this is not a suburban house, but rather a latticework garden pavilion lightly set on a brick parapeted terrace.

The low horizontal roof that covers the bedroom wing creates a series of interior small cubicles reminiscent of a ship's cabin, whereas the higher exposed gable roof of the living-dining room presents a more public space. This space, as with many of his midwestern and eastern Usonian houses of the time, has the usual long built-in couch next to the fireplace, above which is a long and narrow horizontal band of windows where natural light penetrates the patterned wood screens. The dining space projects into one of the glass bays overlooking the adjacent terrace. The kitchen work space is treated in Usonian fashion—as a diminutive work center tucked in behind the mass of the brick fireplace.

In his autobiography Wright sets down nine design features he considered essential to his thirties ideal of the Usonian house. These range from "Visible roofs are expensive and unnecessary," to "Furniture, pictures and bric-a-brac are unnecessary because the walls can be made to include them or be them." His Usonian house was a distillation of the California ranch house then coming into vogue, the openness of plan, which he had so successfully introduced into his Prairie houses of the 1900s, and the desire and need in the Depression years to build modest-sized dwellings. The small scale of his thirties Usonian houses perfectly matches the scale of the most popular of American house types of the time, the Cape Cod cottage.

Wright, of course, meant far more in his use of the term Usonian than that of a description of these small, single floor houses; Usonian in his mind was synonymous with organic, with democracy, and the suburban and rural dispersal of people.

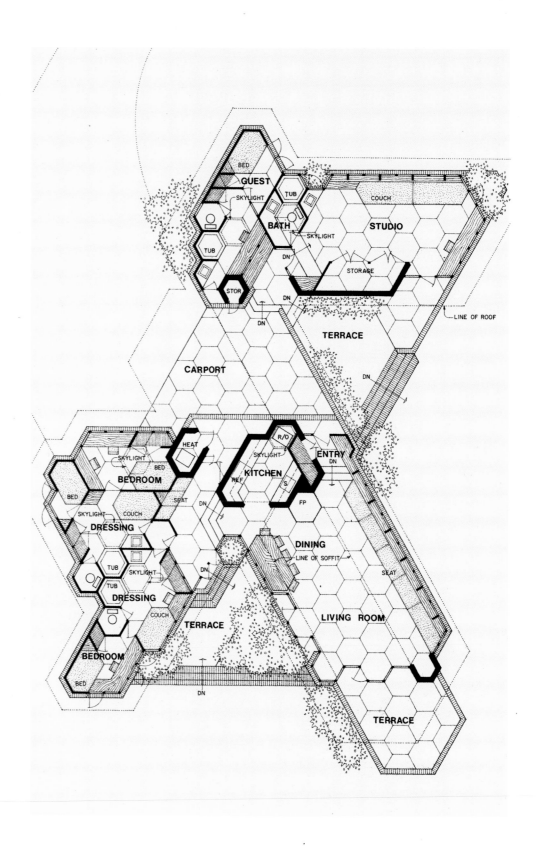

GEORGE D STURGES HOUSE

Fascination with the symbol of speed was one of the dominant qualities of design and architecture of the 1930s. In its popular vein, the Streamline Moderne captured this spirit through curved surfaces, exaggerated horizontal lines, pipe railings, portholes, and semitransparent walls of glass brick. Wright absorbed and then expanded on this theme directly in his 1936 Administration Building for the Johnson Wax Company at Racine, Wisconsin. In the Sturges house, as he had so elegantly accomplished in the Kaufmann house, Falling Water, he abstracted this sense of speed one or two steps further.

The Sturges house, with its form theatrically cantilevered over the hillside, plays off the drama of rapid motion with an Arts and Craft approach that evokes a finely crafted streamlined sailing yacht of the 1930s. The small scale of the interior, reinforced by the architect's furniture and the dark horizontal redwood walls held together by cadmium-plated screws, presents a variety of conceptual and visual games: from the strong hint at the interior cabin of a streamlined yacht to that of a cabin associated with a turn-of-the-century Craftsman interior, and finally to a symbolic expression of the machine (in image and fact). Additional play is apparent in the contrast between

the sense of solidity the brick provides on the entrance side of the building and the hovering quality of deck, balustrade, and the row of glass doors that dominate the street side.

Though in no sense as romantically situated nor as sumptuous in budget as Falling Water, the Sturges house arguably represents the architect's most abstract expression of his attachment to the ideals of speed and movement of the 1930s.

ARCH OBOLER GATEHOUSE AND STUDIO-RETREAT

*I*n 1940, Wright projected one of his most spectacular California designs, Eagle Feather, a house for Arch Oboler. The site was a theatrical one, high on a mountaintop ridge surrounded by surrealistic rocky outcrops interspersed with native chaparral. The view from this ridge is of the coastal community of Malibu far below and of the Pacific Ocean spread out beyond. Regrettably, the main house was never built, but other segments of the complex were completed. These consist of the stone and wood gatehouse (1940) and a small pavilionlike studio-retreat (1941).

The lightweight impression given by the wood walls and cantilevered roofs of these two buildings contrasts with their earthbound, rough stone walls underneath. The long wall extending from the gatehouse conveys, in an abstract way, the atmosphere of the walls of a Near Eastern Arabic castle.

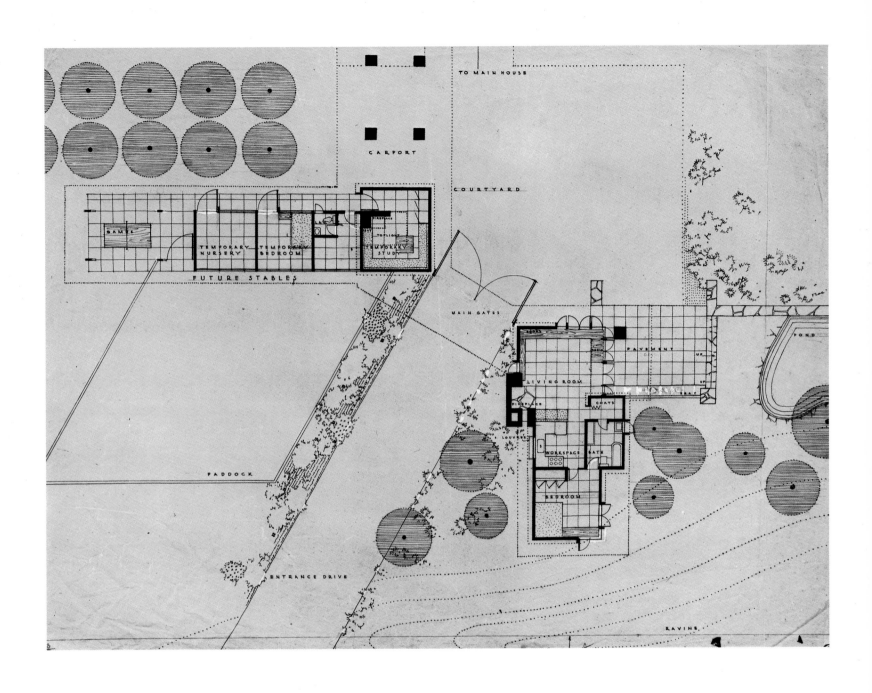

TO MAIN HOUSE

CARPORT

COURTYARD

GAMES

TEMPORARY
NURSERY

TEMPORARY
BEDROOM

TEMPORARY
STUDIO

TOPLIGHT

FIREPLACE

FUTURE STABLES

MAIN GATES

POND

PAVEMENT

LIVING ROOM

FIREPLACE

COATS

LOUVRES

WORKSPACE

BATH

PADDOCK

BEDROOM

ENTRANCE DRIVE

RAVINE

In its use of materials and projecting forms, the design of the gatehouse and studio reiterated a theme Wright was pursuing in other projects accomplished during this period, especially in his Rose Paulson house in Phoenix, Arizona (1940) and the John C. Pew house in Madison, Wisconsin (1940). This theme was the use of masonry as a transition and connection between the natural site and the lighter wood surfaces and forms of the building above. The masonry base is an extension of the site; the building hovers over it.

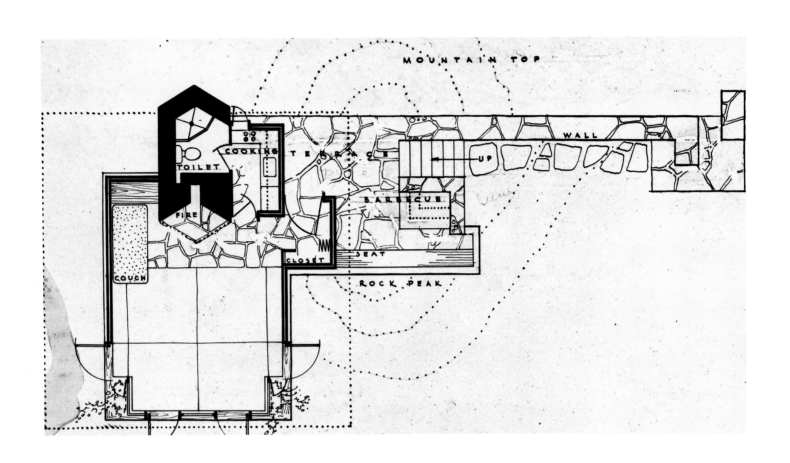

MOUNTAIN TOP

TOILET

COOKING TERRACE

FIRE

COUCH

CLOSET

SEAT

BARBECUE

WALL

UP

ROCK PEAK

MRS. CLINTON
WALKER
HOUSE

*I*n 1954, Wright said of this house, "The over-all effect is quiet, and the long white surf lines of the sea seem to join the lines of the house to make a natural melody." Situated on the rocks overlooking Monterey Bay, the house, with its floating blue-colored metal roof and the pointed prowlike form of its stone terrace, indeed resembles a ship being readied for sea. The dramatic, yet harmonic relationship of the house to its setting expresses Wright's own language of the organic—a oneness with the site—as well as the sympathetic hand of landscape architect Thomas D. Church.

Although now somewhat enlarged, the house when built was quite small, only 1200 square feet including the carport. Within this space, Wright organized a variation on his Usonian plan: a living-dining room centered around a fireplace, utility kitchen core, and off this a galleried wing containing three bedrooms and their baths. The plan is based on a module of four-foot interlocking equilateral triangles composed as one might assemble a jigsaw puzzle. The interior feeling of the bridge of a yacht is captured in the small scale of the spaces, the detailing, and the furniture, which was almost all built-in.

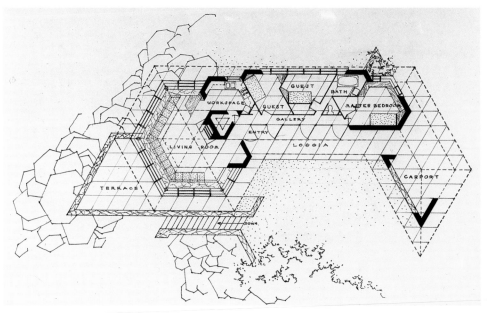

MAYNARD P.
BUEHLER
HOUSE

In the years immediately after World War II, Wright elaborated frequently on his theme of the Usonian house. Though always arranged around a tight and compact masonry core, these houses were often enlarged and loosely spread out over their sites. In plan and concept his Usonian houses of the 1940s and 1950s in California are almost identical to those designed for the Midwest and East. These Usonian houses emerged then as a type, like his earlier Prairie houses. Shared universal qualities tied these houses together even though accommodations were sometimes made to the specifics of site, variations were made to meet client needs, and in some cases materials native to the site were used.

The Buehler house is a characteristic example of these post-1945 Usonian designs. Its walls are of conventional manufactured concrete block, which are countered by the lighter feeling of wood for doors, windows, and the thinness of the roof planes. The plan is that of a single story, L-shaped configuration, with an obliquely angled living room. A terrace defined by low concrete block walls includes the swimming pool. The pool is situated adjacent to the long wing of bedrooms, which open out to the pool and terrace on the same level.

V. C. MORRIS
GIFT
SHOP

*L*ong and quite rightly acknowledged as one of the gems of twentieth century American architecture, the small Morris store beautifully illustrates how Wright could take a mundane building type, that of the small retail shop, and adroitly maneuver it into an architectural monument.

The narrowness of Maiden Lane encouraged Wright to deal both reticently and dramatically with the facade of the building. The building's wall of fine narrow bricks, with accentuated horizontal raked mortar joints, is a pleasurable surface close up, and is also effective when seen at a slightly oblique angle from down the street. The tour de force is the great splayed Romanesque arch, which first catches attention and consequently lures one inside. In this theatrical arch, one encounters a motif used earlier by H. H. Richardson, Louis H. Sullivan, and by Wright himself in the early 1900s (for example in the Arthur Heurtley house of 1902 in Oak Park, Illinois) and later (in his unrealized schemes of 1925 for Sugar Mountain). A subtle treatment of lighting also serves to draw attention to the entry, especially at night: a vertical band of small rectangular lights and a horizontal row of lighted glass bricks march to and terminate at the centerline of the arch.

Within, Wright included a circular ramp similar in basic concept to that used for the Guggenheim Museum in New York (1942–1956). The merchandise displayed in the shop could be seen in glass enclosures, through circular openings, and from various vantage points on the ramp.

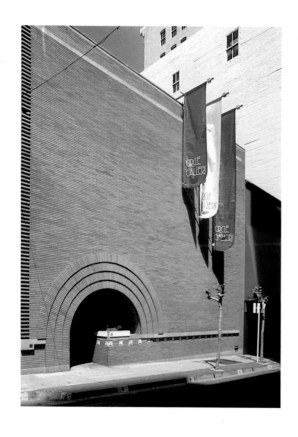

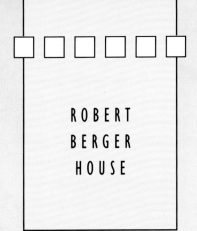

ROBERT
BERGER
HOUSE

*I*n design, the Berger house presents a variation of Wright's 1930s Usonian house. The fireplace and the work-space kitchen constitute a central masonry core. Off to one side is the living-dining room, and projected off the other is the bedroom wing. Externally, the customary extended low-pitched hip roof protects the glass walls below.

The house appears to emerge naturally from the ground by the use of heavy, form-built walls of native rock and concrete. A stone and concrete parapeted walled terrace in the form of a pointed ship's prow extends off the living room. Even the family dog is provided with his own Usonian doghouse, attached to the house and roofed in a fashion similar to that of the dwelling.

The house was detailed and designed so that it could be built by its owner, and it has been carefully and beautifully carried out. Its low forms, and especially the use of native rock, fit in well with this hilly, partially forested section of Marin County above the San Francisco Bay.

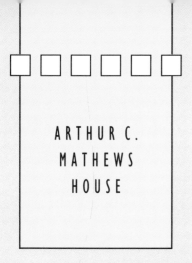

ARTHUR C. MATHEWS HOUSE

The plan of the Mathews house is based on a diamond formed by doubled equilateral triangles. Geometric configurations—squares, circles and segments of circles, triangles, and hexagons—came increasingly to dominate Wright's work from the late 1930s on. The living room wing and the bedroom wing opposite are extended out so as to create a partially enclosed private terrace and garden. The flat terrain of the site is taken, in a classical Wright mode, as a major theme in the design of the house and its terraces. The walls of horizontal raked-joint brick and the accompanying horizontal bands of wood windows and glass doors are carried up to the wood soffit of the low-pitched, hipped roof. From his earliest designs of the 1890s on, Wright used the masonry chimney mass to provide a sense of permanence, and in the case of this house and others, to gather and hold a loose composition together.

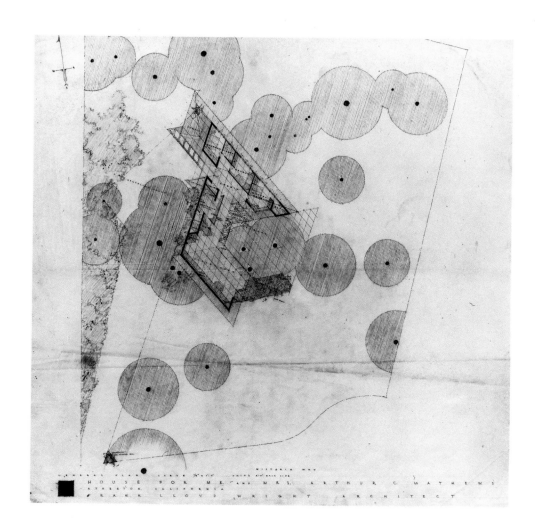

WILBUR C. PEARCE HOUSE

A group of Wright's post-World War II Usonian schemes were based on the use of segments of a circle. In these schemes an inner circular wall was generally articulated by a row of glass doors, and behind these doors ran an open garden room, which served as both an informal living space and as a corridor. The covered entry and carport in these houses usually occupied one end of the segmented curve; the opposite end was devoted to bedrooms; and the central area encompassed the living room, dining room, and kitchen (or as Wright labeled it, the work space).

Wright first employed these segmented designs in the second Herbert Jacobs house (Middleton, Wisconsin, 1944) and later in the Laurent house (Rockford, Illinois, 1949). In these houses and in the Pearce house, the L-shaped configuration of the classic Usonian house is maneuvered into a C-shaped configuration, with the interior of the curve housing an outdoor courtyard living space. The Pearce house appears as the logical end product of this Usonian type. With its location atop a foothill ridge of the San Gabriel Mountains, the house enjoys views towards Los Angeles and the ocean, and to the northern mountains. For this reason, large areas of glass were placed on both sides of the house. The walls are concrete block, a material Wright had used in the twenties and then extensively in the years after 1945. The curved walls of the house and the entrance carport are shaded and visually pulled to the ground by a projecting flat roof whose wide faccia creates an exceptionally strong terminating line.

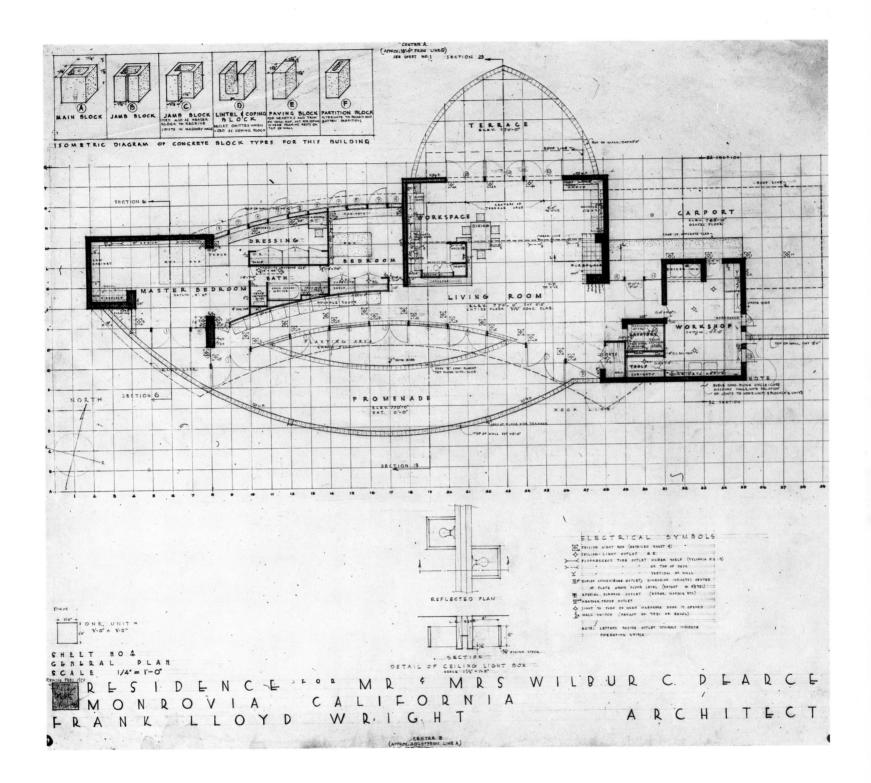

ISOMETRIC DIAGRAM OF CONCRETE BLOCK TYPES FOR THIS BUILDING

RESIDENCE FOR MR & MRS WILBUR C. PEARCE
MONROVIA CALIFORNIA
FRANK LLOYD WRIGHT   ARCHITECT

ANDERTON COURT SHOPS

This solution of providing for a series of small shops was Wright's conceptual suggestion of how a shopping center, large or small, might be designed. His approach was to build vertically and to connect the four levels of shops and offices by means of a ramp. To emphasize the ramp, Wright winds it around a raylike "science fiction" mast, a mast that also succeeds in dramatically advertising the presence of the building. The narrow, open ramp system, together with a small sunken garden, appropriately suggest both an urban and suburban atmosphere.

Later changes, a canopy on the top level and inappropriate signage, presently compromise the design. Still enough remains of Wright's concept for a suburban vertical shopping center to illustrate what he was trying to accomplish.

KARL KUNDERT
MEDICAL
CLINIC

Though the size and the scale of the building is domestic, the high clearstory, punctured by patterned wood panels, and the character of the public approach to the building intimate its medical office use. Both externally and internally the warm wood ceiling and detailing, along with the brick walls, create a quiet and restful series of spaces. The principal interior space, the patients' lounge area, opens out on two sides to the patio through a series of folding wood doors. The patio itself is partially screened by a wall, and on one side it faces onto San Luis Creek.

Wright's initial design for the building was in patterned concrete block, but this could not be realized because of local building code restrictions. His translation of this first scheme into brick and wood, though less insistent, was nonetheless highly successful.

Close to the town's center, the siting of the building on the edge of a creek and within a grove of trees denies its urban location and suggests instead a countryside setting.

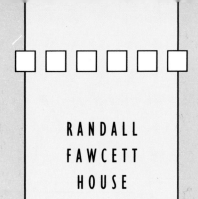

RANDALL
FAWCETT
HOUSE

*T*he emphatic, almost overstated, horizontality of the Fawcett house effectively mirrors the landscape of this section of the San Joaquin Valley. The plan, that of an expanded U with a carport-shop wing, is arranged around a low-walled garden and adjacent swimming pool. A shaded, partially roofed loggia that faces northwest provides the entrance. The living room, as the public and family great hall, occupies the center of the dwelling. Intimacy of space is introduced into this great hall by a secluded inglenook, which adjoins a cavelike fireplace.

The house is constructed of concrete block, each layer slightly stepped inward. The sheet metal roof is dramatically cantilevered, and the extended soffit is cut into angular jagged holes through which light casts an ever-changing pattern on the walls and terrace floors below. Within, this jagged quality is repeated in cut-out wood screens, lighting fixtures, and other details. The interior exhibits Wright's usual array of both movable and built-in furniture.

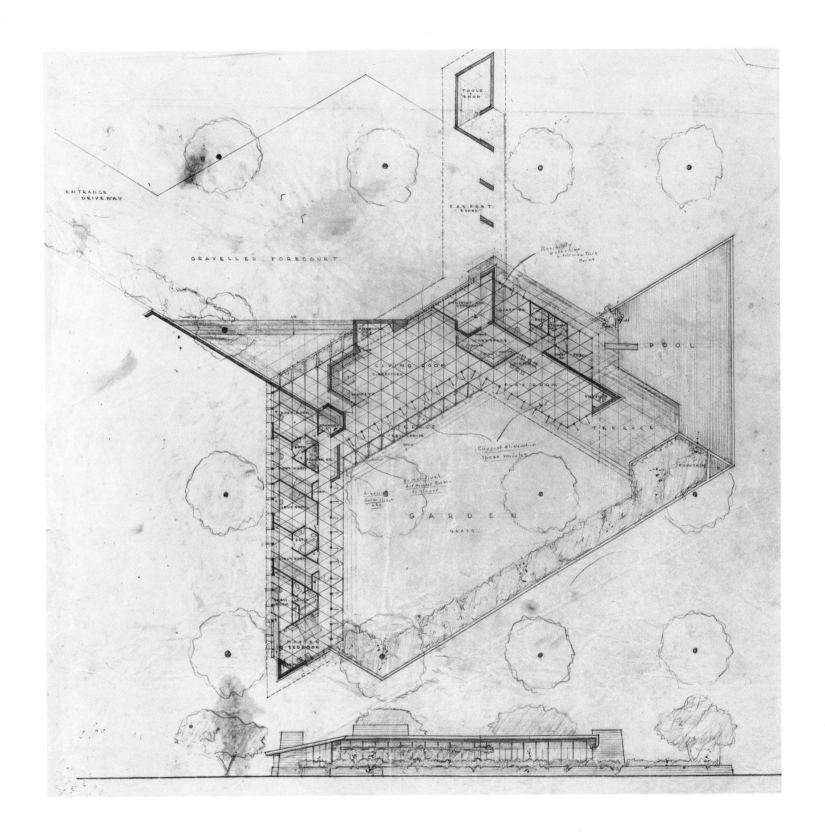

ROBERT G.
WALTON
HOUSE

The Walton house brings together a number of Wright's earlier domestic themes. The rectangular L-shaped plan is an enlargement of his classic Usonian house of the late 1930s, especially that of the first Herbert Jacobs house at Madison, Wisconsin (1937). Other elements, such as the use of concrete block (including patterned "Usonian block") and the parapeted flat roofs, look back to his early California work of the 1920s. The long narrow gallery leading to the bedrooms and the high, centrally placed kitchen, which is part of the fireplace mass, hark back to his work of the 1930s. Externally the design is composed of three parts: a central core with parapeted walls; the living room articulated by a regimental row of perforated concrete block piers and topped by a wide stucco faccia; and the extended low-roofed bedroom and playroom wing.

Both the movable and built-in wood furniture reinforce the rectangular 90-degree premise of the house. The dining room chairs, with their high open backs, are an abstracted version of similar chairs Wright designed as far back as the 1890s.

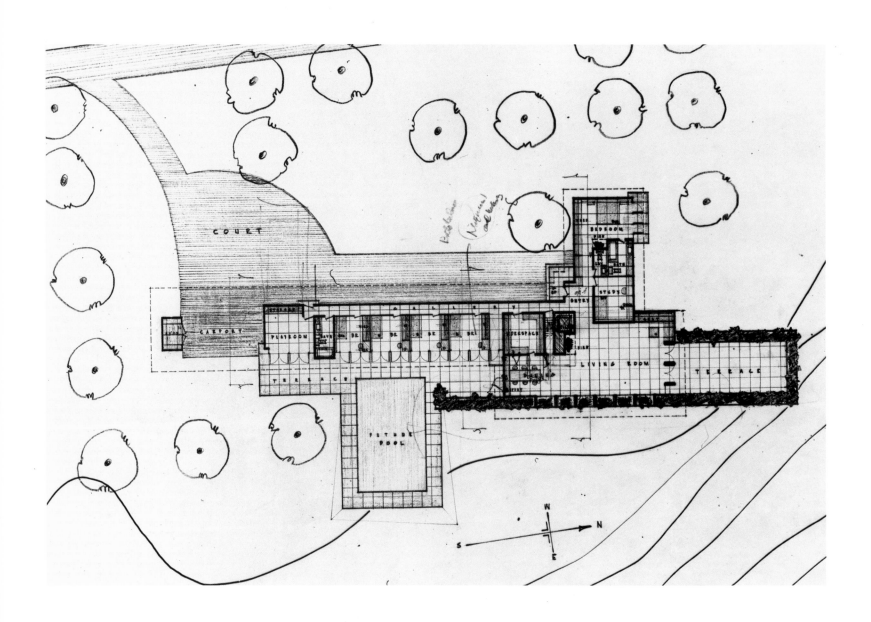

GEORGE ABLIN HOUSE

1958
2460 Country Club Drive
Bakersfield

The Ablin house is situated on a slightly rising knoll in the suburban country club district of Bakersfield. Essentially, it is a classic fifties Wright suburban dwelling, adjusted to the specifics of site, view, and climate of the warm inland San Joaquin Valley.

The plan of the house is based on a variation of Wright's triangular module (with some modification). The walls are concrete block, including patterned perforated block for windows, visually held in place by low-pitched, wood-shingled gable roofs. The roofs extend outward to provide shade for the window walls, terraces, and the long entry walkway. The covered walkway leads to a central, tent-like pavilion that houses the entry, living room, dining room, and the high-ceiling kitchen "work space." Two low wings extend out from this central pavilion: one includes a study and master bedroom; the other, the children's playroom and bedrooms. The low concrete parapet walls that define the living-dining room terrace and the swimming pool terrace effectively shut off the suburban view below, forcing one to be aware of the openness and expanse of this section of the great inland valley. Within are a number of examples of Wright's free-standing wood furniture.

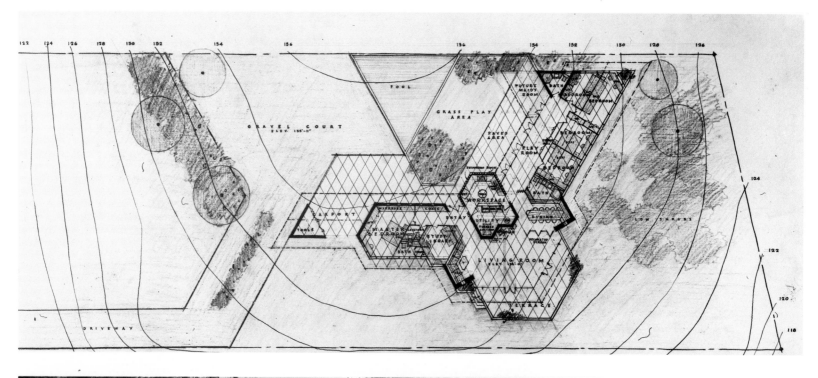

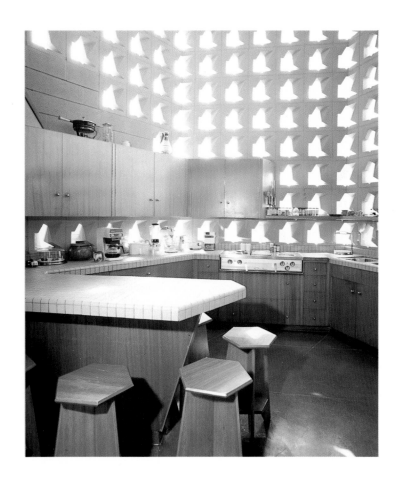

MARIN COUNTY CIVIC CENTER

The Marin County government complex was under design and construction at the time of Wright's death in 1959. The buildings were finished by Aaron Green as associate architect, together with William Wesley Peters and the Taliesin Associated Architects. The Administration Building was completed in 1962; the Hall of Justice in 1969; and the Veteran's Memorial Auditorium in 1972. This complex of buildings carries over into the 1950s Wright's 1930s involvement with the popular Streamline Moderne image as a symbol of the machine and, by implication, of the future.

From the freeway, the two bridgelike structures, with their low arches seeming to spring from their hills, suggest several themes. At once, the visual impact is futuristic—a Buck Rogers science fiction city on a far planet; at the same time it suggests a gigantic Southern California motel and restaurant. The passage of the internal roads under the structure takes the International Style view of buildings, roads, and the urban environment, with its ideological attachment to the mechanical, and transforms it into an informal, romantic suburban world.

Wright's ideal of the city, Broadacre, is evident in the complex; buildings are a miniaturization of essential parts of this city planning scheme he conceived in the mid-1930s. The Civic Center should also be seen as a direct expression of Wright's view that in a democracy, it is the citizen and his activities that count. The narrow, skylighted interior atriums, which are public, the Board of Supervisors auditorium, and the importance placed on the library reinforce the sense of this being a citizen's "civic" center rather than a bureaucratic government center. Wright's landscape design, including a small meandering lagoon, still needs to be fully realized to fulfill what he had in mind for this vision of America, as a universal middle-class society.

PILGRIM
CONGREGATIONAL
CHURCH

The design for this church, finished shortly before Wright's death, consisted of four parts: a prow-shaped, tentlike sanctuary, an adjacent chapel, church offices, and a fellowship hall. These sections were drawn to terminate in a central stone tower surmounted by a thin metal spire. The building structure included a rough stone and concrete base, with the upper metal roofs suspended from rows of high-pitched precast concrete "poles." (The much needed tower has not been built, and the thin pencil-like quality of the hovering concrete poles seems not to have been carried out in the final building.) The plan is based on Wright's triangular module; here, this triangularization effectively provides an inviting, low-winged entrance facing the parking area. Wright's usual sensitivity to site is apparent in the way he comfortably united the building to the small hill it is placed on, and in the sympathetic rapport he created between the masonry walls and the stony, wooded setting.

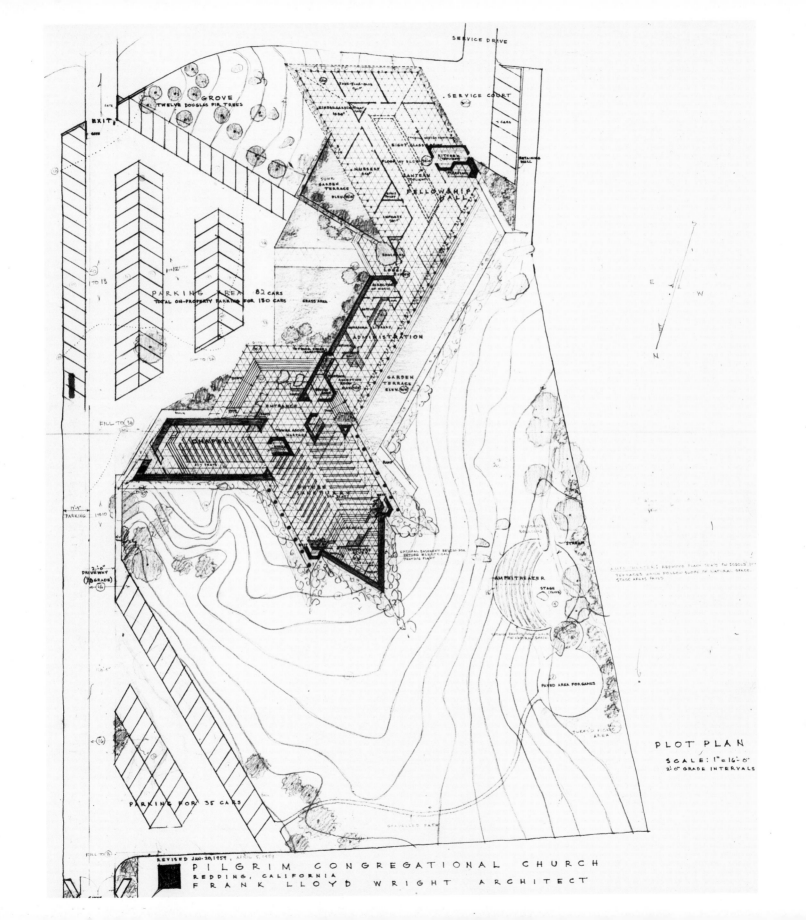

PLOT PLAN

SCALE: 1"=16'-0"
2'-0" GRADE INTERVALS

REVISED JAN. 29 1959, APRIL 5, 1959

PILGRIM CONGREGATIONAL CHURCH
REDDING, CALIFORNIA
FRANK LLOYD WRIGHT ARCHITECT

HILARY AND JOE FELDMAN HOUSE

Wright died in 1959, but buildings and houses based on his unrealized designs are still being built by the Frank Lloyd Wright Foundation. No matter how well such designs are carried out from the working drawings, questions inevitably arise as to whether or not they should be realized, and if so, whether they should be considered as designs by the architect. Wright did indeed arrive at specific design themes and then work out variations on them, yet his practice was a continually evolving one. Thus, it is highly doubtful that he would ever have taken a late 1930s design and produced it unaltered in the mid-1970s, as is the case with the Feldman house. There is also the question of on-site supervision during construction, which on occasion could modify a design considerably. Finally, if Wright's organic, site-specific approach to design is to be believed, a scheme for one client and one site could not easily be moved to another without violating his approaches.

The Feldman House appears to overcome some of the difficulties of building a Wright design many years later; one must say that the Feldmans have added to our architectural heritage. From the unrealized work of the architect, they selected the 1939 design for the Lewis N. Bell house, intended for a site in west Los Angeles, and set it down in a wooded

section of Berkeley where it has the appearance of being completely at home. The design is a late 1930s Usonian scheme of hovering thin horizontal roof planes that contain the redwood the brick walls below. Towards the street, one of the cantilevered roofs presses out to cover the entrance and carport; the living and dining rooms open to a brick terrace on the garden side of the house.

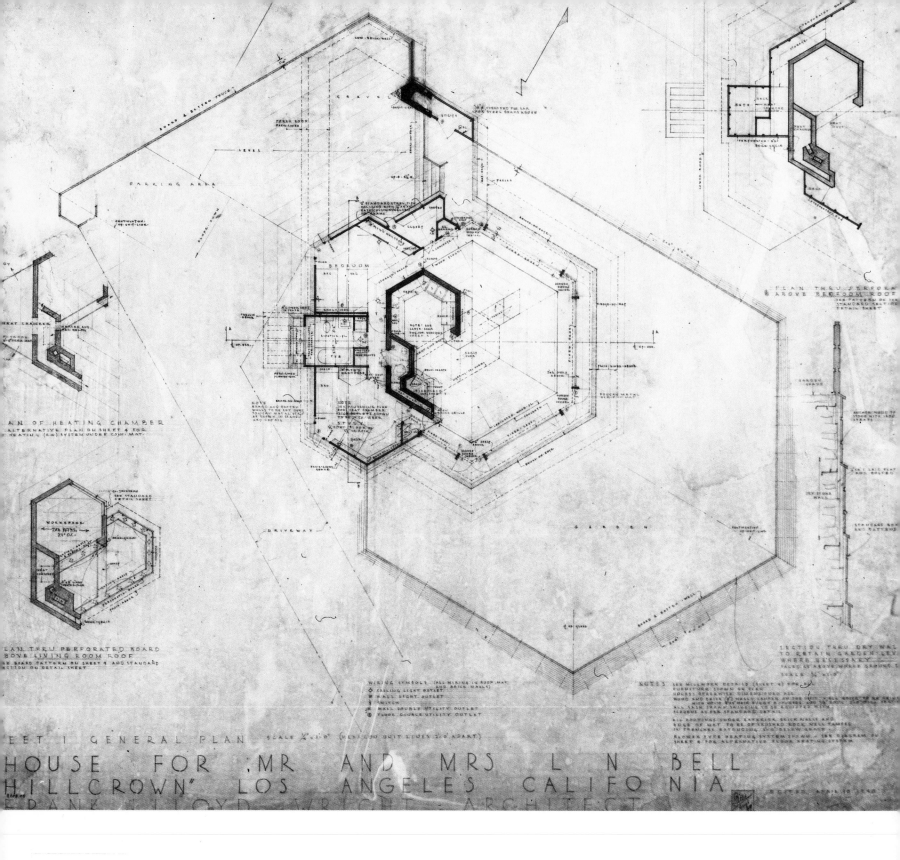

SHEET I GENERAL PLAN   SCALE ⅛"=1'-0" (HEXAGON UNIT LINES 2'-0 APART)

HOUSE FOR MR AND MRS L N BELL
"HILLCROWN" LOS ANGELES CALIFORNIA
FRANK LLOYD WRIGHT ARCHITECT

Wright's unrealized California projects often reveal as much or even more about his approach and his reaction to the West Coast as do his built projects. This chronological list constitutes a number of his major projects.

Press Building for the *San Francisco Call,* San Francisco, 1912.

Aline Barnsdall Theater, Artist Studios, Apartments, and Stores, Olive Hill, Hollywood, 1920.

W. J. Weber House, Los Angeles, 1920 (eventually designed and built by Lloyd Wright).

Project for a Cement Block House (client unknown), Los Angeles, 1921.

Edward H. Doheny Ranch Development, Sierra Madre, 1921.

Merchandising Building, Los Angeles, 1922.

A. M. Johnson Desert Compound and Shrine, Death Valley, 1922.

G. P. Lowes House, Eagle Rock, 1922 (eventually designed and built by R. M. Schindler).

Lake Tahoe Summer Colony, Emerald Bay, Lake Tahoe, 1922.

Sachse House, "Deep Springs," Mojave Desert, 1922.

Aline Barnsdall Kindergarten, "Little Dipper," Olive Hill, Hollywood, 1923.

Opposite: floorplan for Lewis N. Bell house, unbuilt. This page: drawing, Press Building for the San Francisco Call, *unbuilt.*

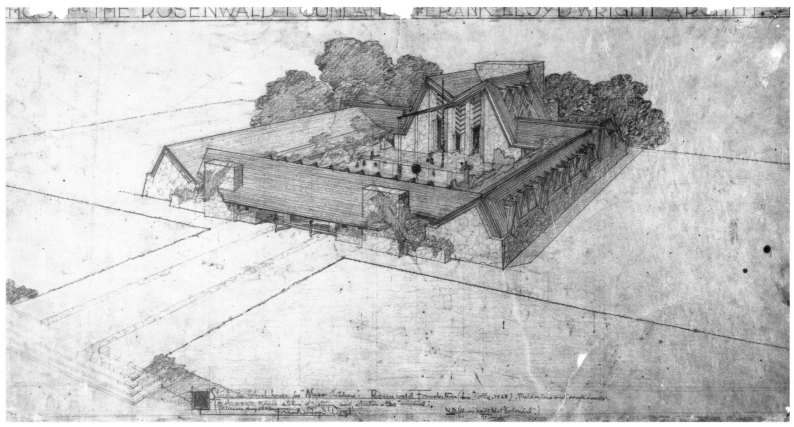

*Above: drawing, Rosenwald Foundation
Schoolhouse, unbuilt.*

Library Building, for Mrs. George Millard,
 Pasadena, 1925 (eventually designed
 and built by Lloyd Wright).

Schoolhouse for Negro Children, for the
 Rosenwald Foundation, La Jolla,
 1928.

Elizabeth Noble Apartment House,
 Los Angeles, 1929.

"All Steel" Housing Development for 100
 Houses, Los Angeles, 1937.

E. A. Smith House, Piedmont Pines, 1938.

Ralph Jester House, Palos Verdes, 1938.

Lewis N. Bell House, Los Angeles, 1939.

Edgar A. Mauer House, Los Angeles, 1939.

Arch Oboler House, "Eagle Feather,"
 Malibu, 1940.

John Nesbitt House, Cypress Point,
 Carmel Bay, 1940.

Stuart Haldorn House, Carmel, 1945.

V. C. Morris House, "Sea Cliff," San Francisco, 1946.

Play Resort and Sports Club, for Huntington Hartford, Hollywood, 1947.

Huntington Hartford House, Hollywood
 Hills, 1947.

Ayn Rand House, Hollywood, 1947.

Nicholas P. Daphne Funeral Chapels,
 San Francisco, 1948.

Concrete Bridge for the San Francisco Bay,
 1949.

Lenkurt Electric Company Building,
 San Mateo, 1955.

Christian Science Church, Bolinas, 1957.

Wedding Chapel for the Claremont Hotel,
 Berkeley, 1957.

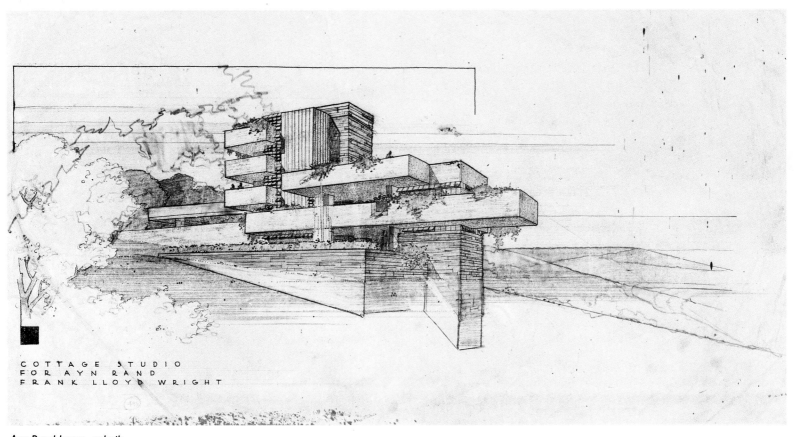

COTTAGE STUDIO
FOR AYN RAND
FRANK LLOYD WRIGHT

Ayn Rand house, unbuilt.

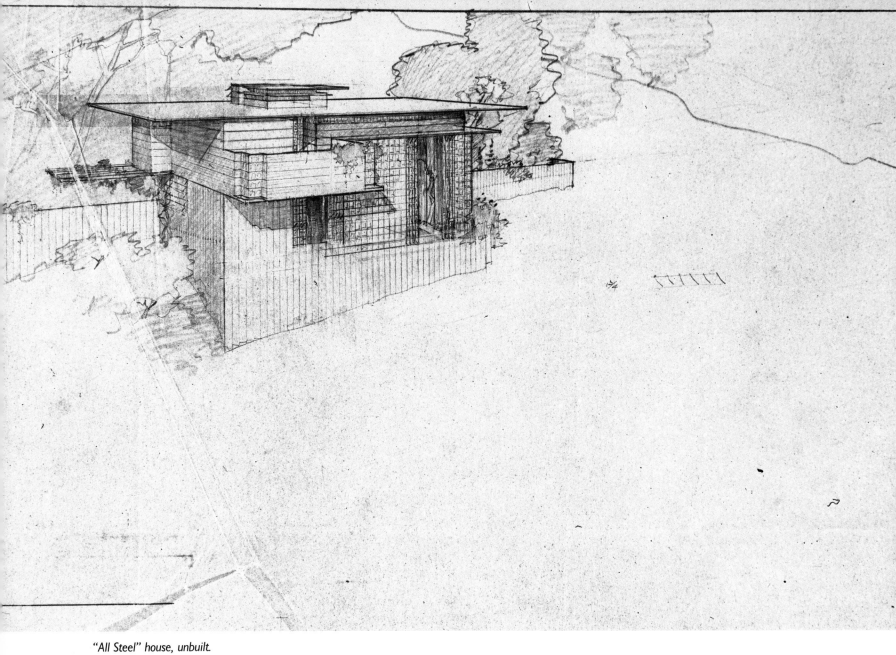

"All Steel" house, unbuilt.

The following books and articles concern Frank Lloyd Wright's work in California.

Architectural Forum. "Frank Lloyd Wright." 68 (January 1938): 1–103.

———. "Work of Frank Lloyd Wright." 88 (January 1948): 65–155.

———. "China and Gift Shop of V. C. Morris, San Francisco." 92 (February 1950): 79–85.

———. "Parasol for the Arts: Veteran's Memorial Auditorium, Marin County Civic Center." 135 (July–August 1971): 5.

Architectural Record. "Marin County Court House, California." 157 (June 1975): 109.

California Arts and Architecture. "Frank Lloyd Wright: The Residence of Mr. & Mrs. George D. Sturges, Brentwood, California." 57 (April 1940): 14–15.

Canty, Donald. "Client's View of the Hanna House, 1936, Palo Alto, California." *Journal* American Institute of Architects 70 (November 1981): 64–67.

Drexler, Arthur. *The Drawings of Frank Lloyd Wright.* New York: Bramhall House, 1962.

Futagawa, Yukio. *Houses by Frank Lloyd Wright.* (Tokyo: R.D.A. Edita, 1975.

Gebhard, David. *Four Santa Barbara Houses, 1904–1917.* Exhibition catalog, Art Galleries, University of California, Santa Barbara, 1963.

Gebhard, David, and Harriette Von Breton. *Lloyd Wright, Architect: 20th Century Architecture in an Organic Exhibition.* Exhibition catalog, Art Galleries, University of California, Santa Barbara, 1971.

Gebhard, David, and Robert Winter. *Architecture in Los Angeles: A Compleat Guide.* Salt Lake City: Peregrine Smith, 1985.

Gebhard, David, Robert Winter, and Eric Sandweiss. *Architecture in San Francisco and Northern California.* Salt Lake City: Peregrine Smith, 1985.

Goldberger, Paul. "A Lasting Wright Legacy." *New York Times Magazine* (June 16, 1985): 54–56, 72.

Hanna, Paul R. and Jean S. *Frank Lloyd Wright's Hanna House.* Cambridge: M.I.T. Press, 1981.

———. "Furnishing Our Frank Lloyd Wright Home." *Frank Lloyd Wright Newsletter* 5:2 (1982): 1–6.

Hitchcock, Henry-Russell. *In the Nature of Materials: The Buildings of Frank Lloyd Wright 1887–1941.* New York: Duell, Sloan and Pearce, 1942.

House and Home. "A Planning Lesson from Frank Lloyd Wright . . . How Big Can a Tiny House Be?" 5 (March 1954): 95–105.

Journal American Institute of Architects. "Hanna House Placed on the National Register, Palo Alto, California." 68 (May 1979): 82.

Kanner, Diane. "Freeman House Deeded to USC." *Los Angeles Times* (March 25, 1984): 34–35.

Kaufmann, Edgar, Jr. "Wright Setting for Decorative Art." *Art News* 48 (February 1950): 42–44.

———. "Frank Lloyd Wright: The 11th Decade: Survey of Works." *Architectural Forum* 130 (June 1969): 38–41.

Levine, Neil. "Hollyhock House and the Romance of Southern California." *Art in America* 71 (September 1983): 150–165.

Life. "The House One Man Built." 47 (December 28, 1959): 92.

McCoy, Esther. "Architecture West: Four Frank Lloyd Wright Textured Block Houses." *Progressive Architecture* 53 (September 1972): 76.

Montgomery, Roger. "Frank Lloyd Wright's Hall of Justice." *Architectural Forum* 133 (December 1970): 54–59.

Progressive Architecture. "Wright Post Office." 43 (September 1962): 76.

———. "Doghouse, Berger House, San Anselmo." 47 (May 1966): 114.

———. "Civic Center Building, San Rafael, California." 48 (February 1967): 30.

Protetch, Max Gallery. *Frank Lloyd Wright Drawings.* New York: Max Protetch Gallery, 1984.

Radford, Evelyn Morris. *The Bridge and the Building: The Art of Government and the Government of Art.* New York: A Hearthstone Book, Carlton Press, Inc., 1974.

Rand, George C. "A Civic Center and the Civitas: Marin County Civic Center, San Rafael, California, A Critique." *Journal* American Institute of Architects 69 (April 1980): 46–57.

Sergeant, John. *Frank Lloyd Wright's Usonian Houses: The Case for Organic Architecture.* New York: Whitney Library of American Design, 1976.

Smith, Kathryn. "Frank Lloyd Wright, Hollyhock House and Olive Hill, 1914–1924." *Journal of the Society of Architectural Historians* 38 (March 1979): 15–33.

Southwest Builder and Contractor. "Local Contractor, Architect Discuss Home Designed by Frank Lloyd Wright Fifty Years Ago." 133 (April 24, 1959): 13.

Storrer, William Allin. *The Architecture of Frank Lloyd Wright: A Complete Catalogue.* 2nd ed. Cambridge: M.I.T. Press, 1978.

Sweeney, Robert L. *Frank Lloyd Wright: An Annotated Bibliography.* Santa Monica: Hennesey and Ingalls, 1978.

Tselos, Dimitri. "Exotic Influences in the Architecture of Frank Lloyd Wright." *Magazine of Art* 47 (April 1953): 160–169.

Twombly, Robert C. *Frank Lloyd Wright: An Interpretive Biography.* New York: Harper and Row, 1973.

Viladas, Pilar. "Invisible Reweaving: A 1923 Textile-block House by Frank Lloyd Wright Is Meticulously Restored by a Team of Patient Perfectionists." *Progressive Architecture* 66 (November 1985): 112–117.

Western Architect and Engineer. "Mr. Wright and His Successors." 221 (March 1961): 20–33.

Wijdeveld, Hendricus T., ed. *The Life Work of the American Architect Frank Lloyd Wright.* Santpoort, Holland: C.A. Mees, 1925.

Winslow, Carleton M., Jr., ed. *Discovering San Luis Obispo County.* San Luis Obispo: California Polytechnic University, 1971.

Woodbridge, Sally. "Wright Restored: The V. C. Morris Store." *Progressive Architecture* 64 (November 1983): 404.

Wright, Frank Lloyd. "In the Cause of Architecture." *Architectural Record* 63 (January 1928): 49–57; (February 1928): 145–151; (April 1928): 35–356; (May 1928): 481–488; (June 1928): 555–561. *Architectural Record* 64 (July 1928): 10–16; (August 1928): 98–104; (October 1928): 334–342; (December 1928): 507–514.

———. "Honeycomb House." *Architectural Record* 84 (July 1938): 59–74.

———. *An Autobiography.* New York: Duell, Sloan and Pearce, 1943.

———. *Drawings for a Living Architecture.* Introduction by Giuseppe Samona and A. Hyatt Mayor. New York: Horizon Press, 1959.

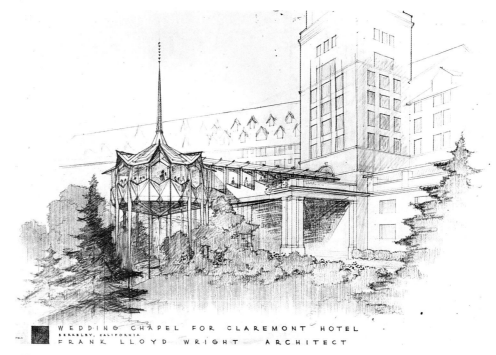

WEDDING CHAPEL FOR CLAREMONT HOTEL
BERKELEY, CALIFORNIA
FRANK LLOYD WRIGHT ARCHITECT

This page: drawing, Wedding Chapel for Claremont Hotel, unbuilt. Opposite: drawing, John Nesbitt house, unbuilt.

Architect and Engineer. "Anent Lloyd Wright Criticism." 107 (October 1931): 82.

Boyd, John Taylor, Jr. "A Prophet of the New Architecture." *Arts and Decoration* 33 (May 1930): 102.

Gebhard, David. *Schindler.* Salt Lake City: Peregrine Smith, 1980. Pp. 37–44.

Hitchcock, Henry-Russell. *In the Nature of Materials: The Buildings of Frank Lloyd Wright 1887–1941.* New York: Duell, Sloan and Pearce, 1942. Pp. 77–78; pls. 245–248, 281–284.

"A Planning Lesson from Frank Lloyd Wright . . . How Big Can a Tiny House Be?" *House and Home* 5 (March 1954): 98.

Levine, Neil. "Hollyhock House and the Romance of Southern California." *Art in America* 71 (September 1983): 150–165.

Tselos, Dimitri. "Exotic Influences in the Architecture of Frank Lloyd Wright." *Magazine of Art* 47 (April 1953): 160–169.

W.P.A. Writer's Program. *Los Angeles: A Guide to the City and Its Environs.* New York: Hastings House, 1941. P. 231.

Wright, Frank Lloyd. "America Tomorrow: We Must Choose Between the Automobile and the Vertical City." *American Architect* 141 (May 1932): 16.

————. *An Autobiography.* New York: Duell, Sloan and Pearce, 1943. Pp. 235, 239, 240.

————. *Ausgeführte Bauten und Entwürfe von Frank Lloyd Wright.* Berlin: Wasmuth, 1910.

————. "Highlights." *The Architectural Forum* 55 (October 1931): 410.

————. "In the Cause of Architecture: I The Logic of Plan." *The Architectural Record* 63 (January 1928): 49.

————. "In the Cause of Architecture: VII The Meaning of Material—Concrete." *The Architectural Record* 64 (August 1928): 102.

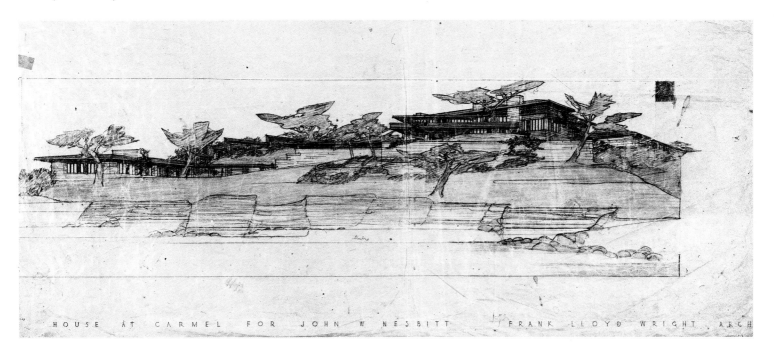

HOUSE AT CARMEL FOR JOHN W NESBITT — FRANK LLOYD WRIGHT ARCH

INDEX

A. D. German warehouse, 3, 23
Adler and Sullivan, 3
Architecture and democracy, 44, 112
Autobiography, 2, 44
Bell, Lewis N., 121
Broadacre City, 6, 112
Cheney, Mamah Borthwick, 9
Church, Thomas D., 59
Como Orchard Colony, 9
Design: concrete, 23, 33, 63, 80, 93, 105,
    117; horizontal lines, 9–10, 33–34, 43,
    75, 93; motifs and materials, 1–6, 38,
    49, 56, 79–80, 93, 99, 105, 117
Doheny Ranch, 4, 7
Eagle Feather, 53
Falling Water, 37, 50
Gill, Irving J., 3
Green, Aaron, 111
Griffin, Marion Mahoney, 9

Guggenheim Museum, 68
Hartford, Huntington, 5
Heurtley, Arthur, 67
Historic influences, 3–5, 23, 26, 34, 53
Jacobs, Herbert, 80, 99
Jacobs house, 37
Johnson, Reginald D., 29
Johnson Wax Administration Building,
    37, 49
Kaufmann, Gordon, 29
Lake Tahoe Summer Colony, 5
Laurent, Louis, 80
Maybeck, Bernard, 5, 29
Midway Gardens, 3, 23
Obler, Arch, 5, 53
Offices, design of, 89
Paulson, Rose, 56
Period Revival, 3
Peters, William Wesley, 111

Platt, Charles A., 3
Prairie Style, 1, 10, 44, 63
Retail shop, design of, 85
Rew, John C., 56
Richardson, H. H., 67
Ross, Charles S., 9
Smith, George Washington, 3, 29
Streamline Moderne, 49, 111
Sugar Mountain, 67
Sullivan, Louis H., 67
Taliesin, 37, 111
Usonian house, 6, 43–44, 59, 63, 71, 79–
    80, 99, 122
von Holst, Herman, 9
Wasmuth portfolio, 2, 9
West, Martin Eli, 30
Wright, Eric, 30
Wright, Lloyd, 2, 30, 33, 121